MARGARET BENEFIEL

CRISIS LEADERSHIP

A little book of leadership

Morehouse Publishing
NEW YORK

Church Publishing Incorporated
19 East 34th Street
New York, NY 10016

Cover design by Jennifer Kopec, 2Pug Design
Typeset by Progressive Publishing Services

Library of Congress Cataloging-in-Publication Data
A record of this book is available from the Library of Congress.

ISBN-13: 978-1-64065-437-2 (paperback)
ISBN-13: 978-1-64065-438-9 (ebook)

Contents

Preface

It is one thing to study and write about leadership in a liminal season. It is another thing to live through it.

In the fall of 2019, I published a book called *How to Lead When You Don't Know Where You're Going: Leading in a Liminal Season.* It is a book about leading through seasons of disorientation, when something has ended but a new thing is not yet ready to begin. Little did I know that the world would soon erupt in twin pandemics. The arrival of COVID-19 and a worldwide social justice reckoning threw all of us into deep confusion. A year of political turmoil added to the chaos. The concepts in my book suddenly became painfully personal and real.

Like so many others, my work life hit a wall in the early months of 2020. A well-planned portfolio of consulting and speaking engagements disintegrated overnight as we moved into shutdown. I was suddenly faced with zero income stream and an unknowable future. My initial shock was followed by months of reinvention, the transition of product lines into online formats, and the creation of new content. The year was frustrating, exhilarating, wildly creative, and downright scary.

Early on, I realized that the only way through this crisis was to turn inward—leaning into my own spiritual center for sustenance and guidance. I learned to quiet my frightened spirit, surrender to the inevitable losses, and trust that God would do a new thing through me.

Throughout this season, I was grateful for my training at the Shalem Institute, where five years earlier I had absorbed practices for contemplative living and leadership. At Shalem I learned to yield and to listen for the whispers of divine guidance. Relying on my Shalem training, I found my way through the murkiness of painful endings and through the confusing early months of the in-between experience.

Looking forward, I believe that we will be in a liminal state for some time to come. We may be re-engaging some familiar old practices now. However, the unsettledness of this season will be with us for a while. There are more losses to be sustained and many new discoveries still ahead. We are not yet ready to claim a new beginning. And we are desperately in need of spiritual guides who can stand with us in our disorientation: mentors who will show us how to embrace our own unraveling and how to discover what lies on the other side of letting go. Margaret Benefiel, the executive director of the Shalem Institute, is one of our proven guides. This text is a welcome roadmap for weary travelers who still have "unlearning" to do.

The book you are about to read is a thoughtful compilation of lessons from a handful of courageous leaders. Individuals who negotiated crisis by embracing contemplative leadership practices. Each case study begins with a personal reckoning—if my organization and I perish, so be it. From this stance, each leader encourages their followers to deepen discernment practices, discover new ways to serve, engage new opportunities within the chaos, and transcend previous limitations. Spoiler alert: remarkable things happen along the way!

Throughout this text, Benefiel is a faithful steward of the stories offered and the lessons learned. Her wisdom shines through this text, garnered from decades of experience as a leadership coach and spiritual director, and punctuated with the insights of a seasoned manager and leadership educator. Enjoy the read.

Susan Beaumont
author, coach, consultant, and spiritual director

Introduction

Three major crises in 2020 plunged me into reflecting on leadership in new ways. This little book on crisis leadership grew out of my own self-reflection on leadership and organizational life, plus out of learnings from leaders I interviewed and read about. Dr. Anthony S. Fauci, director of the National Institute of Allergy and Infectious Disease, and Jonathan Reckford, executive director of Habitat for Humanity, are public figures with enough material written about them that I could learn lessons from their leadership by drawing from articles I read. All the other leaders in this book I interviewed. As I listened to my own experience and that of others, chapter themes emerged.

Chapter One: "Yikes!" begins by expressing my own experience when COVID-19 hit and made its dreaded impact on the Shalem Institute, where I serve as executive director; it was followed closely by the police killing of George Floyd and the time of racial reckoning in the United States, which was followed closely by a bitter pre- and post-election season. The chapter then notes the dire straits that many other leaders and organizations found themselves in at this time.

Chapter Two: "If I Perish, I Perish" examines the importance, in crisis leadership, of building on the paradoxical foundation of letting go: both letting go of the need for personal survival and letting go of the need for organizational survival.

Chapter Three: "Stay in Liminal Space, Grounded in the Storm" examines liminality, that uncomfortable place in which we find ourselves when the old ways have disintegrated and the new have not yet emerged. It considers the importance of staying in the liminal space long enough for next steps to emerge naturally.

Chapter Four: "Dive Deep and Discern" considers how leaders can dive deep into their spiritual practices in order to stay in the liminal space and let go of survival needs. Spiritual practice leads naturally to discernment, a rich resource for decision-making in times of crisis.

Chapter Five: "Surface to Serve" explains how a focus on mission and service keeps the eye on the ball in times of crisis and leads to clarity about what needs to be done.

Chapter Six: "Don't Waste a Good Crisis" uses Winston Churchill's maxim to examine the ways that a crisis suspends the status quo and makes new breakthroughs possible.

Chapter Seven: "Transcend and Include" focuses on organizational development and the ways crises can bring breakthroughs in organizational structures that weren't possible before.

While the chapters build on one another as the stories of the leaders highlighted in the book unfold, each chapter also stands alone. The reader may read the book from start to finish or dip into a chapter whose theme is of interest. The chapters and subsections provide bite-size chunks that, on their own, provide help for the busy leader facing crisis.

1 ▪ Yikes!

Mid-March of 2020, we found ourselves facing a rapidly spreading pandemic that suddenly forced our staff at the Shalem Institute to work from home. Just three months earlier, while on a retreat that focused on an upcoming move, we had discerned that working from home wouldn't work for our staff. Our shared meals, brainstorming meetings, lunchtime walks, and the easy back-and-forth among our workstations were all things that contributed to community and productivity. Yet here we were.

Furthermore, we had just canceled our pilgrimage to Italy and our pilgrimage to Iona, and postponed another major program, which meant a loss of $115,000 of expected income—over ten percent of our annual budget. Then the retreat center hosting our annual board/staff retreat called to cancel our late March retreat; the gathering that we counted on for community-building, creative ideas, deep prayer, and discernment: gone. As executive director of Shalem, I lay awake in bed at night obsessing, "Yikes! When will this hemorrhaging stop? I'm letting Tilden (our founder) down. I'm letting God down."

We grieved. We grieved the loss of our in-person office work environment, our lunches together, our celebrations of work achievements, birthdays, and personal milestones. We grieved the loss of our pilgrimages to beautiful places—"thin places"—with good food and deep community. We grieved the loss of our in-person program residencies at retreat centers nestled in rolling countryside, with nourishing food, prayerful connection, and good fun. Heartbreaking as it was for me, I had to tell the person who was slated to begin as our new director of operations that the future looked uncertain and I would understand if he decided not to take the job.

Then, police killed George Floyd in late May, protests erupted, and the United States was faced with a racial reckoning, a call to face our original sin of racism. As an organization supporting contemplative living and leadership, helping people discern how contemplation and action manifest in their own lives, we were starkly confronted with the pandemic of racism in our country. We had to ask, "How are we complicit in this? And what is ours to do?"

As protests increased and the U.S. election neared, bitter political rivalries sharpened. Tempers flared. Then the election occurred, taking days to resolve, with the ripple effects lasting far longer. Exacerbated by a sitting president making baseless claims of election fraud and doing everything in his power in the two months following the election to overturn the results, the divisions in the United States widened. Violence broke out in the streets. Rioters stormed the U.S. Capitol, forcing a shutdown of Congress's certification of the election results. We asked again, "What is ours to do?"

Far from unusual, our story at Shalem mirrored that of many others, each with its own unique aspects stemming from the mission and DNA of each organization. In the short span of ten months, our lives were turned upside down. We were quarantined. We knew people who had COVID-19. We knew people who died from it. We wondered if we had it. Some of us did. We worked from home, or we lost our jobs. (Unless we were essential employees, in which case we were exposed to the virus daily.) We felt the financial impact. We felt the loss of freedom. We felt fear. We felt sadness. We felt grief.

As a two-week prohibition on in-person gatherings stretched into two months, six months, and as of this writing, ten months, with no clear end in sight, leaders in all settings struggle. Businesses have closed, churches limp along, schools reopen then close again, nonprofits seek to reinvent themselves. Furthermore, leaders wrestle with responding to racism and responding to a bitterly divided country. This was not the world that these leaders anticipated when they took their jobs. This was not what they signed up for. The world changed dramatically in a matter of months. Leaders (if they still have their jobs) ask, "What is mine to do? What is ours to do? Will I survive? Will we survive? Does that matter?"

Reflection Questions

1. What have been the "Yikes!" moments for you in your leadership experience?

2. What do those moments reveal about your attachments?

2 ▪ If I Perish, I Perish

So there I was, along with billions of others around the world, wondering if I would survive the pandemic. And there I was, along with millions of other leaders, wondering if the organization I led would survive. But preoccupation with my own survival wore thin quickly. Even if I only had a short time remaining, I wanted to use that time well. And being preoccupied with Shalem's survival got old quickly. Even if Shalem had only a short time to live, I wanted to help it live fully during its last days on earth. I wanted to step back, face reality, and look at the bigger picture.

Facing reality meant I had to admit that, despite taking all precautions, I might contract the virus. I might die from it. Facing reality meant I had to admit Shalem might go under. If that happened, I would lose my job, and all the employees for whom I had responsibility would lose their jobs.

I remembered the words of Queen Esther, "If I perish, I perish" (Esther 4:16). We are all mortal—not only individuals, but also organizations. I might die from the virus. Shalem may not survive a long siege. While I had to do my best to take personal precautions and safeguard my health as best I could, my ultimate task was not personal self-preservation. My ultimate task was serving in the world as I am called to serve. And while I had to be a faithful steward of the leadership responsibilities entrusted to me, my ultimate leadership task was not to perpetuate the institution I led. My ultimate task as a leader was serving the greater good, serving God. In the big picture, I was but one small thread in the tapestry of humanity. In the big picture, Shalem was one small thread in the tapestry of all the good work in the world.

Furthermore I had to remember that I was human, too. As a leader, I felt fear, sadness, anger, and grief, just as those I was leading did. I needed to give myself permission to feel all my feelings. I needed people with whom I could be vulnerable and cry. I needed time for spiritual practice, to be held in the great Love that was beyond me, beyond the virus, beyond this time in history.

"If I perish, I perish" served me well in addressing the pandemic of racial injustice as well, and the unsteadiness and instability of our country's moorings during the pre-election and post-election chaos. Self-preservation was not the highest good, nor was perpetuation of the institution of Shalem. If I felt called to take risks for the sake of justice, for the sake of democracy, I wanted to respond faithfully, not letting fear for my safety or my job hold me back.

Again, my situation was not unique. Leaders in business, churches, education, health care, and nonprofits all struggled with the same thing. We all had to do our best to take care of ourselves, while at the same time acknowledging that personal self-preservation was not the highest good. And we all had to act responsibly in our leadership roles, discerning the next step and faithfully walking in it, while at the same time acknowledging that perpetuating our institutions was not the highest good. If our institutions could not adapt to the new world in which we found ourselves, it was time to ask, "Have we served our purpose in the world? Is it time for us to disband and let others carry our work forward?"

Stuart Higginbotham, rector of Grace Episcopal Church in Gainesville, Georgia, also found "If I perish, I perish" to be a foundational principle during the crisis of the pandemic. Early on, he noticed that his biggest challenge was navigating his own anxiety. As he reflected on the massive level of anxiety he felt, he realized that he took on others' fears because he was afraid that church meant so little to people that if he didn't respond to their every concern they would leave. The pandemic had laid bare an assumption he had been carrying unconsciously. A church already in decline might be encountering its death knell, so it was up to him to save it. Furthermore, if the church died, there were personal consequences. He would lose his job and would be seen as a failure. That burden weighed heavily on him: "I felt like the fate of the institutional church rested on *my* shoulders."

Once he realized the enormous weight he was carrying, he knew he needed to let go. If the church was doing to die, it would die. If he was going to lose his job, he would lose it. Once he came to terms with those possibilities, he was able to stop, look, and listen for what *was* actually arising:

> If I can sit still long enough and be quiet, amazing things are happening all around. What is mine to do in the midst of all this? How am I being present? What my people need me to do right now is to be present. What inner work do I need to do in order to be more present?

As he kept turning his anxiety over to God, he was able to serve his people by being present and holding the space for them to feel their feelings. He asked himself, "What would happen if, in meetings when people got distressed, instead of trying to fix it, I just acknowledged it and said, 'I know. It's really sad.'" He experimented with simply holding the space, ready to let the church die if it had served its purpose and no longer had a role to play in the new world in which it found itself.

Conclusion

The paradox of leadership in a crisis is that leaders can lead well only when they give up attachment to self-preservation and to the preservation of their institutions. While a leader might hold tight the notion that trying hard to save the institution will increase the likelihood of its survival, the truth actually lies in the opposite direction. To focus on saving the institution is a self-defeating proposition because institutions are created to serve; when the focus moves from mission to self-perpetuation, the death knell sounds soon thereafter.

Furthermore, when leaders lead with an awareness of their own mortality and that of their institutions, they help the people they lead be their best selves. When people know that their leader puts mission first, they follow eagerly, even in hard times. With their people at their best, leaders can experience creativity, connection, and hope even during crises. Teams and organizations can be who they are called to be and do what they are called to do. Letting go of the need to survive, both personally and institutionally, opens the door to new possibilities. And these new possibilities lead to new life and growth.

Reflection Questions

1. What helps you let go of attachment to personal and organizational survival?

2. How does reflecting on your own mortality free you for more effective leadership?

3. How does reflecting on your organization's mortality free you for more effective leadership?

3 ▪ Stay in Liminal Space, Grounded in the Storm

While I knew that letting go of attachment to my own survival and to the perpetuation of Shalem was the first step, I also knew that I needed to know the next step. I had no roadmap. Our strategic planning process had not anticipated this scenario in our wildest imaginings. Part of me felt tempted to devise a plan, any plan, to chart a course through this storm. Yet another part of me knew I needed to wait even though our old way of doing things wouldn't work anymore. The old was falling apart before our eyes. The new had not yet emerged. Prematurely rushing to devise a plan, I sensed, would prove counterproductive.

I knew I needed to listen. I needed to help hold the space for our staff team to listen. I needed to help hold the space for our board to listen. Just because we couldn't offer programs in our old tried-and-true ways didn't mean the Holy Spirit had stopped working. We needed to listen for what the Spirit was up to in our new circumstance.

Two resources helped me. Otto Scharmer, in *The Essentials of Theory U*, describes the process of "letting go" as one sheds habitual ways of knowing and acting, gradually opening one's mind, heart, and will.[1] Once the shedding is complete (or as complete as any human can ever manage), one must wait with open mind, heart,

---

1. Otto Scharmer, *The Essentials of Theory U: Core Principles and Applications.* (San Francisco: Berrett-Koehler, 2018).

and will to "let come" what will. The "letting come" can't be rushed. The mind, heart, and will must remain open in the midst of the unknowing, for the fullness of what is next to emerge. The process challenges all our ego attachments. While not easy, it provides both an opportunity for personal growth for the leader and the best way to exercise effective leadership in the organization one serves.

Susan Beaumont, in *How to Lead When You Don't Know Where You're Going*, describes "liminal space": the space between the old and the new.[2] She captured our reality perfectly in her description of what it is like when the old disintegrates and the new has not yet come. Our human will has a bias toward returning to the old or rushing to the new, and is profoundly uncomfortable in the liminal space. Yet it is liminal space that provides the holding environment for gestation. Waiting in the liminal space provides room for creativity and growth.

These two resources helped me recognize the normalcy of what we were experiencing. They helped me stay in the uncomfortable liminal space and invite others into it as well. Others had traveled roads like this before. COVID-19 was new, but the experience of living in liminal space was not. The degree to which we could stay in that space with open, listening minds, hearts, and wills would determine the degree to which we could respond to the emerging future waiting to be born through us.

I also found a role model for this process in Dr. Anthony S. Fauci, director of the National Institute of Allergy and Infectious Diseases since 1984. Inspired by his courageous leadership in the

---

2. Susan Beaumont, *How to Lead When You Don't Know Where You're Going*. (Lanham, MD: Rowan & Littlefield, 2018).

COVID-19 pandemic—in the face of libel, scapegoating, death threats, and threats toward his grown children[3]—I dug deeper to learn more about him. I learned that during the AIDS epidemic of the 1980s and 1990s he had exhibited an extraordinary ability to live in liminal space.[4]

As a doctor who specialized in rare diseases and repeatedly discovered ways to cure his patients, Fauci had grown accustomed to success. When the AIDS epidemic hit, he experienced failure after failure. No matter what he tried, his patients kept dying. The tried-and-true drug trials upon which he had always relied for testing new medications for his patients proved slow and cumbersome in responding to AIDS. Activists targeted him as the wall preventing breakthroughs in research and patient care.[5] Going from hero to villain overnight, Fauci faced his reality. In the crisis of the AIDS epidemic, his old methods had broken down. A new way forward had not yet emerged. He could have easily clung to his old ways in the name of science. But instead, he said, "These guys, they dress crazy and they say terrible things, but . . . let me think about this for a minute: If I had a disease in which the result

3. Emma Newburger, "Dr. Fauci Says His Daughters Need Security as Family Continues to Get Death Threats," CNBC, August 5, 2020, https://www.cnbc.com/2020/08/05/dr-fauci-says-his-daughters-need-security-as-family-continues-to-get-death-threats.html.

4. Tim Murphy, "America, Meet Tony Fauci. HIV/AIDS Activists Have Known Him a Long Time," The Body Pro, March 20, 2020, https://www.thebodypro.com/article/tony-fauci-md-coronavirus.

5. Diane Bernard, "Three Decades Before Coronavirus, Anthony Fauci Took Heat from AIDS Protestors," *Washington Post,* May 20, 2020, https://www.washingtonpost.com/history/2020/05/20/fauci-aids-nih-coronavirus/.

was that I would die no matter what, and the government was telling me, 'You can't try anything that might work under any circumstances,' I'd be ramming down the doors, too."[6] When he put himself in their place, he realized he would have made the same demands.

Fauci re-examined everything he had held dear. He lobbied for new protocols for drug testing. In the messy in-between time, he had many questions: Would these new drug trials be scientifically credible? What about the ethics of giving one person a placebo and another person the new drug when the new drug promised to be highly effective? If that proved unethical, how could they test and approve the new drug?

AIDS activists had confronted Fauci about irrelevant drug guidelines. For example, a person taking one drug was forbidden from entering a study for another drug. If one drug kept a person from going blind and another promised to extend the person's life, how could one choose between the two? During the scourge of AIDS, restrictive protocols had dire consequences. Persuaded by these facts, Fauci became an activist within the government to change protocols, which threw him into liminal space for some time as the bureaucracy resisted. Unflinchingly he challenged the status quo, keeping AIDS drug testing in flux for extended periods as he negotiated testing protocols that would better serve the community affected.

---

6. Dave Davies, "Long Before COVID-19, Dr. Tony Fauci 'Changed Medicine in America Forever,'" NPR, April 16, 2020, https://www.npr.org/sections/health-shots/2020/04/16/834873162/long-before-covid-19-dr-tony-fauci-changed-medicine-in-america-forever.

Conclusion

Like letting go of attachment to our own survival, staying in liminal space may feel counterintuitive. Most leaders have a bias toward action; we want either to return to the old ways that worked before or to quickly adopt a new roadmap so we can feel like we're moving. Yet returning to the old or prematurely adopting a new plan will prove illusory if we have not waited long enough in the liminal space, opening our minds, hearts, and wills to the emerging future. As we discovered at Shalem, and as Fauci discovered during the AIDS epidemic, returning to the old or rushing to the new is counterproductive in a crisis. We must stay in the liminal space, with all its messiness, until the new begins to emerge.

Reflection Questions

1. When have you lived in liminal space?
2. What helps you stay in liminal space when you're tempted to bolt?
3. What fruits have you seen come from staying in liminal space?

4 ▪ Dive Deep and Discern

Staying in liminal space and holding on to the larger perspective that saw beyond self-preservation, for both me and for Shalem, required diving deep in prayer. I had a history of my own practice of contemplative prayer, and Shalem was founded in it.

Contemplative prayer is a practice of silent prayer that tries to set aside the ego and await the presence of God. It often begins by focusing on something simple—a word or phrase, for example—and repeating that until the presence of God is felt. Its goal is to connect with God while releasing or transcending, as far as possible, the assumptions and attachments that tie us to the world as we understand it. Diving deep, for us, meant using that familiar spiritual practice to let go of attachments to self-preservation and institutional perpetuation, and to open ourselves to what might emerge through discernment.

Diving Deep

Our weekly staff meetings already began with twenty minutes of contemplative prayer, followed by time for intercessory prayer and prayers of gratitude. Our groundedness in prayer helped us discern what to speak about and how much to speak, and when our speaking served the good of the whole and when it merely served ego needs. When we got off track, we gently returned to the prayerful frame of mind. These practices served us well in staying in the liminal space and listening for what was emerging. In addition, our staff members had their own personal spiritual practices.

The groundedness and wisdom they brought from the fruit of their practice fed into our time gathered as staff.

Our board meetings also started with a substantial period of contemplative prayer. Board members, like the staff, were accustomed to sensing God's presence in the midst throughout the time of working together. Committees and program teams worked in the same way. The practice of diving deep in contemplative prayer had always helped us shed our attachments. In Scharmer's terminology, we shed our habitual ways and moved into open mind, then into open heart, then into open will.

When the pandemic hit, we needed this practice more than ever. When the retreat center canceled our March board/staff retreat, we were bereft. We knew we needed time together in prayer as staff and board, but we didn't know how to get it. Then Katy Gaughan, one of our staff, challenged us to do the retreat on Zoom. The rest of us wondered, "How can we do a whole weekend on Zoom and include the prayerfulness, the experiential and interactive tone, the community-building?" With Katy's help, we got to work imagining, praying, and creating.

The retreat exceeded our expectations. It was indeed an experience of diving deep in prayer: We spent time in prayer individually, time in pairs, time in small groups, and time together as a whole group. We named our losses and grief and let go of our attachment, as best we could, to the things we had lost. We held one another in community, and we let God hold us. We moved from our attachment to the way we had always done things to open mind, open heart, and open will. We stayed in the liminal space, feeling our feelings and sharing our sadness, waiting for the new to emerge.

Again, we were not alone. Other leaders, with the practices that were familiar to them, also discovered ways to dive deep in the crisis of the pandemic to find ways to shed their attachments and live in the liminal space, each in the unique ways springing from their own DNA.

Sarah Willie-LeBreton, provost of Swarthmore College, for example, had to dive deep to get beneath the surface anxiety, frustration, and grief of the faculty, students, parents, and staff during the pandemic. Staying on the surface, reacting to all the emotions, resulted in her feeling annoyed with all the expressions of anxiety. Going deep helped her stay grounded in her values and the values of the institution. It also helped her hear the wisdom contained in the complaints and frustration expressed. She depended on her spiritual practices to help her go deep and hold the space for others to express their frustration. She learned to hold her faculty and students and listen, rather than react, when they offloaded their anger and grief. She learned to accept people in their fear and anxiety. In the spring of 2020, when she saw half the faculty on the boxes of her Zoom screen with their eyes wide in fear and their lips trembling, she knew she needed to speak to their emotions as well as to their rational questions and arguments. She needed to be a non-anxious presence while anxiety ran high. She encouraged her associate deans to do the same: "Part of the role is comforting and challenging and providing an ear for our different constituent groups. Being a container for the anxiety of others is part of the job."

Diving deep helped Willie-LeBreton stay in touch with her heart, with her values, with her mission. And it helped her listen to others' hearts, beneath whatever emotions they presented on the surface. She returned to her spiritual practices and her values again and again, emphasizing the need to balance what could be seen as competing values. By diving deep, she stayed spiritually grounded and was able to relate to others from a place of compassion and values.

Julie Pennington-Russell, senior pastor of the First Baptist Church of Washington, DC, has had to meet a series of challenges since she came to First Baptist in early 2016, with COVID-19 and the time of racial reckoning in the spring and summer of 2020 being but the two most recent. For her, diving deep has meant learning to still herself, go within, and wait in God's presence. It has been only after she has come to this place of stillness that she has heard God's voice, God's call to action. She has had to learn to lean back into the heart of God first, rather than immediately leaning forward into anxious action.

She has found this to be an important practice to bring to the church, as well. Situated in downtown Washington, DC, First Baptist has historically been a church of movers and shakers. Presidents Harry Truman and Jimmy Carter worshipped there. Government, business and nonprofit leaders, lawyers, doctors, and bankers comprise much of the lay leadership of the congregation. While the gifts these leaders bring contribute immensely to the congregation, they can also become tools of the ego. Learning to lean back into the heart of God to allow God to show them how to use their gifts, rather than trying to take charge and figure everything out themselves, is becoming an important spiritual practice for these leaders.

The experience of diving deep also is helping some of the more experienced members of the congregation find a renewed sense of purpose. Years of living and working in DC easily leads to cynicism, and as these members are learning to dive beneath the surface machinations of DC life and are experiencing the fresh springs of God's Spirit, God is reminding them that their purpose in life still awaits fulfillment. God still delights in them and their gifts, and eagerly waits to work in and through them.

The experience of diving deep is serving younger members of the congregation, as well. Many young idealists come to DC eager to change the world and soon find themselves hitting walls, becoming disillusioned, and burning out. As they receive the invitation to dive deep, some of these younger leaders are learning how their activism can be rooted and grounded in God. As their actions flow from that deep connection with God, God sustains them and keeps them resilient in their important work in the world.

For Pennington-Russell and First Baptist, facing these challenges is leading to new birth and a deeper life in God. She sees both the danger and the opportunity inherent in crises play themselves out. A renewed sense of purpose continues to arise for both individuals and the congregation as a whole. For these gifts of the time of crisis, Pennington-Russell is deeply grateful.

Diving deep led, for us at Shalem and for others, to discernment, or, in Scharmer's words, to "letting come." Listening together in prayer leads to a sense of what comes next. Both individual and communal discernment play a part in hearing what is emerging.

Discerning

What is discernment?[7] From the Latin word, *discernere,* meaning "to separate" or "to distinguish" or "to sift through," comes the English word "discernment." Discernment involves "sifting through" interior and exterior experiences to know which ones help one

---

7. These five paragraphs are a further development of part of what I wrote about discernment in *Soul at Work* (New York: Seabury Books, 2005), Chapter 4.

stay present to God and to others and which pull one away from that presence.

Spiritual discernment is a process of going deeper. It is drawing on one's whole self, heart, mind, soul, and spirit. It includes and transcends intellectual analysis. It includes and transcends emotional intelligence. It is the bringing together of all of one's faculties within the larger context of the transcendent. In spiritual discernment, one distinguishes the real from the illusory, the wheat from the chaff. Through being deeply spiritually grounded, the discerner cuts through the usual distractions and attachments that obscure accurate perception and seeks to see reality clearly.

Spiritual discernment is practiced both individually and corporately. Even when done individually, it is never in isolation. Individual and corporate discernment dance together, hand in hand. Corporate discernment requires prepared hearts and minds of the individuals involved. Individual discernment requires the support of a community, nurturing and grounding the person's spiritual life. Individual discernment also requires the accountability of a community, offering checks and balances to the individual's discernment.

Discernment occurs in the larger context of God's love. God's loving care envelops all, making no distinction between the secular and the sacred. Discernment is about hearing God's call in the midst of where one serves, whatever the context, knowing that God is active even in the midst of the messiest of situations. Hearing God's call and responding to God results in freedom—freedom from the need to please others, freedom from attachment to personal gain. As one hears God's voice in the midst of the cacophony of voices all around, both internal and external, one moves into ever greater freedom.

Over the years, practitioners have articulated specific guidelines for discernment: for preparation, for recognizing impediments to discernment, for the practice of discernment itself. Guidelines for preparation for discernment include nurturing a trusting attitude toward God, learning to listen, prayerfulness, familiarity with scripture, humility, and patience. Widely recognized impediments to discernment include self-interest, self-absorption, self-righteousness, desire for security, attachment to a particular outcome, and desire for certainty. The discernment process itself requires maintaining an open and reflective attitude; an ability to listen to where God might be speaking, including through unexpected people and events; patience in waiting for God's answer; an ability to live with ambiguity; and a willingness to test the discernment by its fruits.

We exercised discernment at Shalem's staff/board Zoom retreat, as we listened and prayed individually, in small groups, and in the whole group. Although we tended to think of ourselves as proficient at discernment and had prided ourselves in knowing how to prepare ourselves for discernment and how to recognize and let go of impediments to discernment, we faced new challenges in the new moment. It had been easy to nurture a trusting attitude toward God when things were going well, but it became harder when it looked like we might be on a sinking ship. Similarly, we found listening prayer and patience easier when we could relax into God, but harder when our anxiety threatened to get the better of us.

Furthermore, we found impediments to discernment cropping up like weeds. Our desire for security, our attachment to programs being a certain way, our desire for certainty all got in the way of open-hearted listening. All had to be shed. In the discernment process itself, we sought to maintain an open and reflective attitude, listening for wisdom through others, especially through those with whom we disagreed. We noticed how easy it was to lose a trusting, open attitude when the discussion turned to money, because those conversations brought up fear and anxiety, and egos easily took over. We had to remind ourselves to return to open-hearted presence. We knew we had to live with ambiguity as we sought to stay in the liminal space. We knew our discernments were tentative and needed to be tested. For example, we didn't know if programs on Zoom would attract any participants and we knew we needed to experiment.

As we discerned, new possibilities emerged. Program staff began to re-envision programs on Zoom and, to our surprise, enrollment increased substantially. The board stepped up and pledged more money, which we used as a matching challenge, and the match was surpassed. Again, Shalem was not unique in the need to practice discernment in crisis.

Gretchen Castle, general secretary of Friends World Committee for Consultation (FWCC), has also had to dive deep and discern in this time of crisis. She was grateful for the Friends' practice of listening deeply to God and discerning, sensing a leading to act out of that place of rootedness and groundedness in God. Because FWCC is a Quaker organization, her team shared this orientation. They have practiced discernment for years, both individually and together. Castle muses, "How lucky we are to have a thoughtful contemplative practice that helps us engage in this way and bring our imagination to the world!"

As she invited her team into listening and discernment, she discovered that they could be comfortable with ambiguity, with living in the liminal space, as they listened for what's next. She realized that part of staying grounded, both for herself and for her team, was rest and self-care in the midst of the enormous challenges of this time. She encouraged self-care and caring for one another among her staff, sending them articles, encouraging them to do what they needed to do to stay grounded. She gave her staff leeway to work when they felt they could, and when fear or anxiety or other distractions were present, she encouraged them to take time away: to take a walk, a nap, a bath, or to call a friend, whatever would help them come back to work again in a different frame of mind. They did not need to tell her when they did these things, and they knew she trusted them to do whatever they needed in order to adapt to the uncertainty and anxiety. She knew that it was only through self-care and deep groundedness and waiting that the team would be able to sense what was theirs to do.

Conclusion

Diving deep and discerning help leaders and teams stay in liminal space and listen for what is emerging. Diving deep keeps them grounded. Practicing discernment together provides a foundation for the work that is theirs to do. It is only when they can stay in the deep place long enough and discern carefully together that they are then ready to surface to work together.

Reflection Questions

1. When did you dive deep, and how did diving deep help you stay grounded?

2. How have you practiced discernment personally as a leader?

3. How have you practiced discernment corporately with your team or board?

5 ▪ Surface to Serve

After diving deep and discerning together, leaders and teams must surface to serve. Listening together with open hearts, open minds, and open wills for what is emerging helps leaders and teams let go of attachment to self-preservation and shifts their focus to service. Discernment helps move the focus to mission, asking the question, "Who are we called to be in the world, and how are we called to serve in this time?"

At an early Shalem staff meeting held on Zoom after we began working from home, Trish Stefanik, a staff member who had been praying about our situation, called us to focus on the needs of the Shalem community. What was ours to do? How could we serve our community at this time? She suggested we send out an email to everyone letting them know we were praying for them and including a link to the video "Changeless and Calm." From that simple beginning, we continued to ask how we were called to serve in the midst of the pandemic.

As the spring and summer unfolded, program team after program team was called to dive deep and discern how to serve their audience. While none knew exactly what would best meet the needs of their potential program participants, all worked hard to experiment with reconfiguring their programs on Zoom. Although a few participants chose to wait until they could be together in person, many more signed up for the re-imagined programs and experienced deep contemplative community online. Enrollment grew substantially. Meanwhile, staff teams responded to feedback and continued to experiment and adapt their programs to the new format.

After police killed George Floyd on Memorial Day and protests erupted and the United States was faced with a racial reckoning, we at Shalem again asked, "What is ours to do?" As we prayed and listened and discerned, next steps emerged. We sent a letter to our community, we moved our final "Contemplative Conversations on Race" series session to Zoom, we offered a "Contemplative Conversations on Race" retreat, and we took the retreat out to the leadership teams of two churches. In addition, we realized we needed to do more internally to work toward being an anti-racist organization. We focused a summer staff development session on becoming anti-racist, and then twenty Shalem leaders took an eight-week course offered by the American Friends Service Committee on "Radical Acting in Faith for White People." We began to look at next steps we could take toward diversity, equity, and inclusion in our organization. With a new program year beginning, we began to consider the staff and syllabi of each of our programs, to discern how we could expand them for diversity, equity, and inclusion.

In the seemingly unending season of bitter partisanship and chaos surrounding the election, we at Shalem felt called to focus our Thursday afternoon Zoom prayer times, first envisioned to hold our country in prayer leading up to the election, on post-election healing. Our Wednesday morning prayers for the world addressed the chaos and pain of the times. On Election Day, we held an all-day prayer vigil. On January 6, the day appointed for Congress to certify the results of the election, we focused on praying for Congress and for the protesters. We planned a prayer vigil for Inauguration Day. The daily Simple Presence Zoom gatherings, continued by Shalem's board president after the March board meeting, grounded us. In times of so much pain, injustice, and chaos, we served our community by supporting trust in the Spirit's movement in our midst. Again, our situation is not unique. Leaders everywhere had to dive deep, to get in touch with the bedrock of their mission, and to discern how to best serve their communities in the face of uncertainty.

When Sarah Willie-LeBreton dove deep, she was able to surface to serve at Swarthmore College. She served the faculty by listening, by encouraging, and by cheering them on, hoping that this would help them to be their best selves with students and colleagues. In the spring of 2020, after listening to much fear and worry, she knew she needed to encourage the faculty. She told them at the end of one meeting, "This is the hardest moment we've been through. Every single one of us is up to the task. But I want to acknowledge how hard it is and what an extraordinary job each of you is doing and how proud I am to be affiliated with all of you." She also served faculty by continuing to listen to them and to learn from them, refining the college's responses to the pandemic so that faculty could better fulfill their jobs of helping students learn.

When she had the opportunity to meet with students, she tried to serve them by reconceptualizing the moment as a sacred challenge that might allow them to inspire future generations of students. She challenged them to find creative ways to keep learning, so that their studies wouldn't be interrupted. She reminded them, "You will look back on this moment and you'll be able to talk to people younger than yourself and tell them, 'You too can go through difficult times and come out on the other side.'"

She served parents by helping them to see the big picture and challenging them to catch the vision of what Swarthmore was seeking to do at the time and to partner with the college in accomplishing it. She held the space for parents to complain. She reminded herself to breathe when they directed their anger or rage at her. When she listened to the fear beneath the anger, she found her voice and spoke with compassion about their values and the college's values. When parents complained in the spring of 2020, she reminded them:

> There is no "gotcha" moment here. We are all trying to figure out what makes the most sense. The reason we're going forward continuing to ask you to pay tuition is that we are ensuring that our essential staff who feed our students, who clean their dormitories, who keep our college safe, continue to have jobs. Furthermore, our decision as a faculty to move to Pass/Fail grading was not about depriving your students of the ability to have grades. It was based on knowing how many of our students are in very difficult circumstances and how uneven the playing field was. And we made that decision out of deep discernment and care for all of our students. One of the most important ways we can partner together—faculty, administration, and parents—is by modeling for our students what it means to go through something unexpected and very, very hard together.

Gretchen Castle oriented her team at FWCC toward service. As the inequities of the world came into stark focus during the pandemic, Castle reflected,

> We keep coming back to Jesus's message of love. We must love one another in the midst of systemic inequality. We

have to give up our selfishness. We have to learn to care about people in other parts of the world who are suffering because we are over-consuming. We have a spiritual imperative to love one another, to bring the kingdom of heaven to earth. I'm very grateful to have this collective Quaker family that shares this vision and this imagination of what the world can be. We don't need to be afraid because God will help us through.

When COVID-19 brought into high relief the inequalities between the Northern and Southern hemispheres, FWCC did fundraising for African Friends, collaborating with Friends Church Kenya and Friends United Meeting in new ways, forging promising partnerships. Aware of the enormous gap between resources and supplies that health care workers in the Northern Hemisphere have at their disposal and resources and supplies that similar workers in the Southern Hemisphere have, FWCC and their partners wanted to support frontline workers. Together they were able to provide personal protective equipment for Friends hospitals and clinics in Kenya and other parts of East Africa. The collaborations have continued to grow.

Sandy Clingan Smith, vice president of marketing for AMSURG, a business composed of 250 ambulatory surgery centers, found that her practice of morning prayer oriented her toward service, which helped her, in turn, orient her colleagues and the team she led toward service in the midst of the chaos swirling around them when COVID-19 hit. When the surgeon general closed down elective surgery early in the pandemic, AMSURG wondered how many of its centers (each an independent LLC) would survive. They wondered whether AMSURG itself would survive.

Instead of becoming preoccupied with survival, the leadership team asked, "How can we best serve our providers and patients in this crisis?" Smith and her team pivoted and became responsible for communicating information to the centers to help them make sound decisions. In order for the centers to stay open, Smith's team had to help them keep doctors, patients, nurses, and others safe. Volumes of information were coming in so quickly from the Centers for Disease Control and Prevention (CDC) that it was a mammoth task to digest it and understand what it meant for their centers, and then to get information out in a form that was usable.

Smith's team reinvented how they communicated with their centers. In the first week, they devised a plan for how to keep their centers safe and communicated it via townhall. They then moved into an agile planning process and sent out a new plan every two weeks. They began sending a daily e-mail with the latest news and resources, and archived them all on an internal portal as a way to provide the latest and most accurate medical information. In addition, they took on the task of communicating in the other direction—to government officials—demonstrating that they were keeping their ASCs safe and convincing the government officials that AMSURG was indeed providing essential services.

The leadership team also focused on how they could offer different services, how they could use their infrastructure to support what was needed in the moment. They realized they could protect their ambulatory service center patients and providers better than hospitals could because they only treated healthy patients, not COVID patients. Their doctors began bringing cases over to AMSURG ASCs because it was easier and safer to schedule operating room time there than in the overcrowded hospitals. Another challenge faced by the ASCs was the shortage of personal protective equipment. AMSURG's procurement group rallied and sourced directly from China, providing each center with the PPE it needed.

As a result of pivoting to get up to speed in providing a safe environment for providers and patients and moving other cases from hospitals to their centers, AMSURG flourished. While their colonoscopies went down by half, their total joint cases had more than doubled by the end of the year. By the fourth quarter, they were back up to full capacity of all procedures and close to their normal volume level. With careful cash management, all 250 centers survived.

Smith's team created a thank-you video at the end of the year, recognizing how everyone in the company had rallied and worked overtime to serve their patients. Smith mused, "When I look back, I'm really proud of the work we did. It also explains why I'm so exhausted, physically and emotionally."

Conclusion

The focus on mission that diving deep in prayer and discernment provides leads to service. Leaders and teams must continue to ask, "Given our mission, what is uniquely ours to do in this time of crisis? How can we best serve our community?" Whenever they find themselves anxiously concerned about self-preservation, they must return to a focus on service and begin again. The degree to which they are oriented toward service serves as a litmus test of how well they are living into what is theirs to do in difficult times.

Reflection Questions

1. What keeps you focused on mission?

2. How have you served in the midst of crisis?

3. Where have you seen fruits of keeping the focus on service?

6 ▪ "Don't Waste a Good Crisis"

"Don't waste a good crisis," admonished Winston Churchill during World War II. A crisis suspends the status quo and makes possible what wasn't possible before. A crisis reveals ways of operating that worked in the past, but which are no longer relevant in the new circumstances. At Shalem, we wondered what we might be able to do in the crisis that we hadn't been able to do before. We wondered which of our old ways needed to be shed in the new circumstances. We knew the Chinese character for "crisis" meant both "danger" and "opportunity." What was the opportunity hiding in this crisis for us? What was the danger? We continued to dive deep and listen, going beneath preoccupation with our own fears and discomfort to the bedrock of God's abiding presence and guidance.

We waited and listened and watched. Our first clue came after our Group Spiritual Direction workshop leadership team re-imagined the April program on Zoom and interest quadrupled. With a hunger for contemplative community during the isolation of the pandemic, participants jumped at the chance to participate in a program with reduced costs and no travel time or expense. A rich and deep experience for participants, even on Zoom, convinced us that an invitation lay before us. The leadership team made plans for the September Zoom Group Spiritual Direction workshop to accommodate even more people, and attendance there jumped to sixty (normally sixteen, limited by the size of the retreat center). A small program for years, Group Spiritual Direction continued to grow by leaps and bounds. With the sky as the limit, the team imagined other components: mentoring, an advanced workshop, perhaps even a long-term program. We added an additional Zoom Group Spiritual Direction workshop in January. We also wondered how we might continue online offerings even after the pandemic ended, and we were able to safely gather in person again. It was clear that this program met a deep yearning in people and that it could expand dramatically.

Leadership development, something with which we had struggled for years and on which we had made only incremental progress, suddenly blew wide open. With an aging program staff, we had known we needed to develop younger leaders, yet mentoring new leaders into existing programs proved difficult because we didn't want to displace our wise elders. We now needed new leaders and we needed them quickly. The Group Spiritual Direction program, for example, with sixty people registered for the September workshop, required fifteen small group leaders instead of our customary four. Plus, adding an extra January workshop that not all of our regular leaders could staff meant we would need even more leaders. We brought on five interns to our September program with the expectation that they would lead groups in January. Especially focused on diversity in age and ethnicity, we mentored the five, giving them opportunities to lead groups under the supervision of experienced leaders. We then asked two more people to intern in January.

Meanwhile, our Young Adult Life and Leadership program, once re-envisioned on Zoom, grew substantially in enrollment. With the largest Young Adult Life and Leadership class ever and the most diverse class of any program in Shalem's history, its opening seminar went deep quickly and rich community formed during the first four-day residency in the spring. The youth and diversity of the participants gave us hope for future board and program leadership. Furthermore, the expanded class afforded more opportunities for leadership development, and we brought on younger, more diverse leaders and mentors.

Meanwhile, we began to notice that working from home had leveled the playing field on our staff team. Of the eight administrative staff, five had been working in the office pre-pandemic and three had been teleworking. At our first all-Zoom staff meeting, one of the remote workers smiled and said, "Welcome, fellow teleworkers!" We noticed and smiled back. After a few months, we really noticed. We were all experiencing the same need to find creative ways to connect through Zoom, creating community as we could.

After the March board/staff retreat, the board president continued the daily morning contemplative prayer gathering we began at the retreat, *Simple Presence*, and invited board, staff, program participants, alumni, and friends to join in prayer on Zoom. Some joined regularly, others occasionally; over the following ten months we averaged an attendance of forty. One member of the group also offered Qi-gong three days a week following the prayer time. For some this became a primary spiritual community during the pandemic. For others it was an opportunity to dip in occasionally to contemplative community, knowing that the daily faithful prayer of this group held them and the world in difficult times. *Simple Presence* also afforded more leadership opportunities and invited new leadership development.

Two board members, both clergy (one of whom served as program director of our eighteen-month Clergy program), volunteered to offer a free retreat in May for clergy who faced impossible challenges in the midst of the pandemic. Nearly two hundred clergy participated—and gave positive feedback. The experience invited us to offer clergy more opportunities for support. Some joined

Simple Presence, either regularly or when they could. Some joined the long-term clergy program which started in August, swelling the ranks to make it the largest and most diverse clergy program class since the inaugural one. Some joined the September Group Spiritual Direction workshop. The new program leaders offered another free clergy retreat in the spring of 2021.

Shalem's annual Gerald May Seminar, in which we bring in a well-known contemplative speaker to give a talk one night and lead a retreat the next day, was slated for mid-May 2020 with Wendy M. Wright. At first, we wanted to cancel, but one staff member challenged us to see the possibilities with Zoom. Wendy, a gifted speaker and retreat leader, felt up to the challenge, so we gave it a try. Again, registrations surpassed the previous year's, and participants reported a stimulating, prayerful experience with a sense of connection to God and to one another.

The eighteen-month Soul of Leadership program had an upcoming four-day residency scheduled in May for the Boston cohort and another in June for the Washington, DC cohort. Both groups had already met in person for other residencies, so the participants looked forward to being together again. We were unsure how well this program would work online; all the programs we had re-envisioned online had been opening residencies or short-term programs. We made the mistake of shortening the May residency out of concern for Zoom fatigue and were met with an outcry. The participants asked to schedule supplemental sessions to make up for the shortened residency, which we did. We learned that Zoom fatigue was mitigated not so much by a compressed schedule, but by a spacious schedule with time for breaks, individual prayer and reflection, stretching and body prayer, and walks in nature. The re-envisioned format on Zoom allowed us to "invite" via YouTube videos two of the authors whose books we used, and it allowed more interaction than merely reading and discussing had previously allowed. One participant offered a "visio divina" for one of the morning prayer times that focused on photos of the retreat center where we had met previously, offering a connection back to our in-person experience at that beautiful location.

Our next opportunity with a group that had already met in person the summer before came with the second ten-day residency of the Spiritual Guidance program in June, a group, with staff included, of thirty-six. With a seasoned staff who knew the program well, many of whom had worked together for more than a decade, the concept of moving to Zoom seemed alien. Bon Secours Retreat Center in the wooded hills of Marriottsville, Maryland had served our groups well, and the ten days in person, including the trans-formative informal conversations during the delicious meals and prayerful walks in nature, seemed integral to the program. The staff wondered how a Zoom ten-day residency could possibly be as prayer-ful as the in-person residencies had always been, and how the doubts and grief within themselves and the class could be overcome.

Grief, anger, resentment, loss, and fear manifested themselves in the staff team as we came to grips with the reality of having to offer the program on Zoom. Only after moving through grief did we begin to feel a glimmer of hope, and then we found waves of grief returning when we least expected them. The ten days together proved rich and fulfilling despite the grieving and glitches. The staff and participants experienced the creative power of the Spirit to touch and transform in the virtual world as well as in person. The participants even worked creatively to put together a lively and fun-filled party on the final night, complete with a talent show and conversation clusters.

Before the pandemic, we had signed a lease to move our office to downtown Washington, DC at the end of August. We looked forward to collaborating with other nonprofits in the building, exploring overlap and complementarity in our work. We looked forward to offering workshops and retreats for professionals in the neighborhood, expanding our reach to populations we hadn't reached before. Now we faced moving during a pandemic. What did that mean? Working from home had become our norm, with solitary trips to the office when the need arose for supplies or equipment use. Instead of dreaming about how our new location would facilitate new relationships, we had to focus on letting go. Since we were downsizing our space, we had already planned to let go of stuff. Now we needed to let go of dreams of new relationships, too. Our move became a time of shedding: Shedding furniture, equipment, old files, accumulated stuff we weren't using. Shedding plans for outreach. Shedding dreams of lunches and happy hours and walks in a trendy downtown neighborhood. We realized our move also provided an opportunity to shed some outmoded ways of storing our electronic files, ways that made it difficult to work from home, so we moved our electronic files off our server and onto the cloud.

Prior to the pandemic, we had made the decision to move the annual October Shalem Society gathering from the greater Washington, DC area for the first time in its history. We had planned to hold this gathering of Shalem alumni in Ohio, where the regional leadership team would plan and host the five-day event. With deep grief over the loss of the experiment of hosting Society in one of our regions, we realized we needed to move the program to Zoom. To our surprise, we witnessed the largest enrollment in the history of the Society, with ninety-five people registered, more than double the enrollment of most of the past gatherings. The reduction in price and the elimination of travel, along with the promise of contemplative community in the midst of isolation, once again proved alluring to many. Participants found the plenary sessions just as rich as at in-person meetings, and the small listening circles reported even deeper prayerfulness and community than usual.

When it became clear that the fall 2020 programs and perhaps even winter and spring of 2021 programs would need to go online, we discerned an invitation for a program that had been stalled. Our Personal Spiritual Deepening Program had had two incarnations, and we had been seeking the next one. As we saw so much longing for contemplative community during the pandemic, we created "Heart Longings: An Invitation to the Contemplative Path," an eight-month program with large group sessions, small spiritual direction groups, and one-to-one spiritual direction. Immediately, forty-four people registered for the first informational call, and soon thereafter thirty people registered for the program itself. With a requirement for spiritual directors and group spiritual direction, we saw another opportunity for leadership development. Drawing on some experienced spiritual directors and experienced group spiritual direction facilitators who had previously led this and other Shalem programs and others who hadn't, we also provided opportunities for newer spiritual directors and newer group facilitators, offering mentoring to those who desired it. With a full class and a stable of committed, faithful leaders, the program launched powerfully and successfully.

The crisis of COVID-19 allowed us to break through barriers that had confined us: expanding Group Spiritual Direction, doing significant leadership development and expanding and diversifying our team of program leaders, manifesting the next incarnation of a program for personal spiritual growth, moving our files to the cloud, making the Shalem Society gathering affordable and accessible, and strengthening working relationships within our administrative staff, not limited by geography.

The second crisis, that of police killings and subsequent protests, a time of racial reckoning for our country, put the United States' original sin of racism front and center. Again, we at Shalem were called to ask, "What is ours to do?" What was the invitation for Shalem in this crisis, both internally and externally? For years Shalem, a predominantly White organization, had been working toward more diversity on its board and staff, with limited success. The time was ripe to work more broadly toward diversity, equity, and inclusion.

We took a number of steps to begin to address this issue. We still have much work to do and we have begun to look at next steps we can take toward diversity, equity, and inclusion in our organization. The crisis of a summer of police violence and the related protests in the United States have provided Shalem with the opportunity to step up and do our work. This second crisis allowed us to break through our complacency as a White organization and name the ways that we were complicit in racism and begin to take steps to become more anti-racist. We have begun a long journey, and I pray that we will have the courage and perseverance to continue.

The third crisis, that of the U.S. election season and then the election itself and its aftermath, called us again to ask, "What is ours to do?" We focused our weekly Prayer for the World and biweekly Prayers for Hope and Healing on the election, and held an election day prayer vigil all day on Zoom. Disturbed by the undermining of democracy before, during, and after the election, we focused our prayers on the good being raised up in our country and all else falling away. Our new "Heart Longings" program held its opening retreat November 6–7, a few days after the election, with the focus "Staying Grounded in the Storm." We wanted to explore how our dismay at what was happening around the election could be turned into productive prayer and action, rather than obsessive anxiety.

In the wake of the election, I watched in shock as the authoritarian playbook unfolded with a president bent on undermining democracy to maintain power at all costs. Never say "It can't happen here," I reminded myself. As I prayed, I had a sense of spiritual warfare, of the good being raised up in poll workers to give them the strength to keep counting ballots in the face of threats, of the good being raised up in judges to give them the courage to reject frivolous lawsuits, of the good being raised up in politicians to stand up for the integrity of election results in the face of a corrupt president, of the good being raised up in ordinary citizens to give them the will and the ability to distinguish truth from falsehood as they listen to the rhetoric of politicians. This prayer felt deeper than a particular election. It was about the heart and soul of the nation. A democracy only thrives when its citizens commit to keeping it healthy. A good nation requires good people committed to truth and integrity standing up with courage for what is right. The crisis of this election season, with all its chaos and corruption, provided Shalem with the opportunity to hold space for prayer for our nation and our world, and to speak up for truth and justice. And Shalem is not unique. Many others discovered ways to "not waste a good crisis," in ways consistent with their own mission and organizational DNA.

Jonathan Reckford, Habitat for Humanity

Jonathan Reckford, CEO of Habitat for Humanity, has faced a number of crises in his fifteen years at the helm of Habitat, and has been able to discern the opportunity in each.[8] Each time, he has had to dive deep in prayer and discernment, holding a plumbline to the mission of the organization as they have discerned how to pivot to meet the challenges of the moment. Soon after Reckford arrived at Habitat, Hurricanes Katrina and Rita hit the Gulf Coast of the United States, devastating entire regions. He ditched his plan to visit Habitat projects around the world in order to focus on the immediate need of rebuilding communities. Reckford saw in the crisis the opportunity for Habitat to move from building individual houses to impacting entire regions. They scaled up significantly, not only building houses but also focusing more broadly on the communities they served. The next opportunity followed close on the heels of the first when the 2008 financial crisis hit, causing foreclosures. Without a need for new construction, Habitat shifted from building houses to repair and rehab, resulting in a new focus on community development.

In the double crises of COVID-19 and the overdue racial reckoning, Habitat recognized the opportunity to collaborate. With layoffs of ten percent of its staff in the spring of 2020 and a voluntary pay cut for senior leaders happening at the same time that the need was greater than ever, Reckford had to find a new way forward. By collaborating with others, Habitat continued to fulfill its mission:

> If there's anything I've learned over the last fifteen years, it's that we must be adaptable to a rapidly changing world.

---

8. Jonathan T.M. Reckford, "Commentary: Leading Change in Crisis," *The Non-Profit Times,* September 3, 2020, https://www.thenonprofittimes.com/npt_articles/commentary-leading-change-in-crisis/.

Just as we found new ways to move forward after many previous disasters, Habitat is adapting to the challenges of COVID-19. We are figuring out how to build homes while staying socially distanced. We are discovering new ways to collaborate with others in the housing market. We also are focusing on our founding principles of faith in action and radical inclusivity as we seek to bring healing to communities where all residents can thrive. Bringing people together, we will continue to build homes, communities and hope.[9]

In 2005, Habitat served 125,000 people a year. Through focusing on community development and collaborating with others via a market-based approach (addressing property rights, land use policies, and access to capital), tens of millions of people around the world have been helped. Habitat, along with its partners, now serves a family somewhere in the world every twenty-one seconds.

Sarah Willie-LeBreton, Swarthmore College

As provost of Swarthmore, Sarah Willie-LeBreton discovered a number of opportunities in the crises of the pandemic and the time of racial reckoning. First, diving deep has helped her listen and revealed to her the importance of communication. Her communication with faculty, students, staff, and parents grew stronger during the pandemic than it was before.

---

9. Paul Clolery, "Habitat Cutting Staff and Expenses Due to COVID-19," *The Non-Profit Times,* April 24, 2020, https://www .thenonprofittimes.com/npt_articles/habitat-cutting-staff-and -expenses-due-to-covid-19/.

Second, Swarthmore struggled perennially with inclusiveness and participation in faculty meetings. Willie-LeBreton knew that a besetting challenge in higher education was the desire of faculty to participate in the governance of the institution along with the board and administration, but a lack of workable processes prevented that from occurring.

When faculty meetings moved to Zoom, the barriers to participation came down. From not having to walk all the way across campus just before or after class, to being able to turn off one's video while eating lunch (faculty meetings are always held over lunch), to feeling welcomed no matter what one's status on the faculty, faculty found that it was easier to attend. Attendance at faculty meetings leaped from 40–70 to 100–220. While visiting faculty and adjuncts previously had been told by department chairs not to come, now a special effort was made to ensure that all were invited. Visiting faculty reported, "I feel included for the first time; I feel like I know what's going on; I feel like part of the group." Willie-LeBreton hopes the faculty committee she co-chairs will consider holding at least some scheduled faculty meetings on Zoom post-pandemic to maintain the level of participation; the sense of inclusion is too important to be lost.

Third, the department chairs and program chairs, a group who met with her and the president twice a semester, asked to see her every week when the pandemic hit. Anxious and unhappy about the changes occurring, they wanted to understand them and they wanted a touchstone with their community. In a time of disconnection, they yearned for connection with the people they knew. With the two associate deans joining, they met on Zoom every week through spring and early summer, and then every other week through the rest of the summer. In the fall, they moved to every third week. Remarkably, despite their exhaustion with Zoom, they *all* showed up for the frequent meetings.

Because of the higher level of participation in faculty meetings and the more frequent meetings with the department chairs and program chairs, Willie-LeBreton has received more input from faculty than she had in the past. She reports the sense that she may be becoming a wiser, better leader in the ability to lean in when necessary and change her mind when convinced—outcomes that would likely have taken much longer to achieve had she not been communicating as regularly and extensively with those groups.

While she admits that the anxious and often hurtful expressions of heightened anxiety have resulted in feelings of both compassion and annoyance with several colleagues, she has, at the same time, learned more from them during this time. She has learned about holding both the annoyance and the wisdom together: "You don't get the latter if you're not willing to put up with the former. Just because it's not easy doesn't mean it's not good." Her big takeaway from both the faculty meetings and the meetings with department chairs and program chairs is that technology can be used for greater inclusivity in shared governance. Furthermore, greater inclusivity results in higher morale among faculty, better decisions, and she hopes it has made her a wiser leader.

Fourth, the crisis of the pandemic opened the door to virtual town halls. While Swarthmore had experimented with town halls in the past, turnout had been consistently small, typically fifteen people or fewer. With the changes forced upon the college by the pandemic, leaders knew they needed to experiment with communicating widely to their various constituencies. They began to hold town halls on Zoom for students, for parents and students together, for faculty and staff, and for alumni. With an overwhelming response to each town hall of three hundred, four hundred, five hundred, even one thousand people, they knew they had struck gold. While not as interactive as faculty meetings simply because of their size, anyone could ask questions via the Zoom chat function. Working with a coach and faithfully practicing her spiritual disciplines, Willie-LeBreton learned to stay in touch with and communicate her deepest values in the face of receiving expressions of frustration, anger, and even hostility. As she listened deeply and reflected back the commitments she heard beneath the complaints and affirmed the implicit values in them, participants felt heard and acknowledged. As a result, even in a pandemic when constituents couldn't meet face to face, relationships with students, parents, staff, and alumni grew stronger.

Fifth, the crisis of racial reckoning in the United States has propelled Swarthmore forward toward fulfilling commitments that had been made years before, but had only been moving forward gradually. The conversation among faculty and students about diversity, equity, and inclusion has become top priority, and the conversations are resulting in significant changes. In early January 2021, eleven faculty members, six of them people of color, were recommended for tenure, a result of much hard work in examining bias in promotion and tenure guidelines and changing the guidelines to become more equitable.

Kara Lassen Oliver, Executive Director of The Upper Room

Kara Lassen Oliver also discovered a number of opportunities in the crises of racial reckoning and the pandemic. First, for years The Upper Room had worked incrementally toward diversity, equity, and inclusion on its staff. When Oliver became executive director in April 2019, she had made moving forward on this front one of her priorities, but progress proved slow. In May 2020, the police killings of George Floyd and Breonna Taylor and the murder of Ahmaud Arbery propelled racism and police brutality to the top of the country's radar. For Oliver, it became an opportunity to lift melanated voices. The Upper Room immediately got to work on developing a website and YouTube channel for the spiritual work of overcoming racism.

After a few cautious invitations to long-term friends and partners, they were delighted that other Black Indigenous People of Color (BIPOC) partners came to them and said, "Hey, I wrote this; would you like to use it?" Many helped create the variety of resources. The guiding question became, "How are you creating daily life with God in the midst of racism and White supremacy?" Oliver mused, "We discovered that people really wanted to partner with us. The response was overwhelming. No one said no. People were so willing." The crisis accelerated their progress on providing anti-racist resources. Then the next question became, "How do we keep this connection with our partners outside the building when we're not in crisis mode?"

The crisis also gave them the courage to ask questions that should have been asked earlier, questions that employees were waiting to be asked. In response to questions about how racism impacts employees, Puerto Rican Upper Room employees, for example, shared vulnerably about colorism and racism in their community. An African American man who worked the front desk wanted to leave work in daylight after the time change, and he and others found a new comfort level with conversation and sensitivity to his need to leave work early. In the midst of Hispanic Heritage month in September, Oliver met with the Latinx staff to talk about a new publishing initiative in Spanish and learned that there were varying levels of discomfort with the term "Hispanic." These conversations might not have happened had this crisis not occurred. Furthermore, the door was opened to talk about how The Upper Room work culture silences people and impacts the equity of hiring processes.

Second, the pandemic of COVID-19 disrupted the distribution of *The Upper Room* magazine, the primary source of income for The Upper Room ministries. More than twenty-two thousand churches subscribe to *The Upper Room* magazine, buying multiple copies and distributing it to their parishioners when they come to church. When people stopped coming to church, Oliver and her colleagues wondered what would happen. Would subscriptions cease? Would *The Upper Room* go under? Most importantly, would their subscribers get the spiritual nurture they needed at this time of being cut off from in-person gatherings at their churches?

Oliver, along with the leader of the magazine publishing unit and the organization's core leadership team brainstormed ways to support their subscribers. They sent out ideas about how to distribute the magazine. They reached out to pastors and inquired about how they were doing in the pandemic and invited them, in small groups, to a one-hour online Sabbath. The response to the Sabbath times was overwhelming among a very diverse constituency. They discovered how tired pastors were, scrambling to maintain some semblance of Sunday worship, pastoral care, and church structure in the midst of a pandemic. Pastors were also heartbroken, they found, because of being unable to visit the sick and dying, to hold people's hands, to hold weddings and funerals. The blessing in the Sabbath time, so many pastors reported, was, "I didn't have to lead. You could have done anything and I would have been happy. It's just so great to be at something I don't have to lead."

Third, while The Upper Room had been developing online courses for a decade, the director of online learning had been facing an uphill battle in helping people catch the vision for them. When COVID-19 hit, she said, "I know what to do." She had already created a course on prayer and worry, so The Upper Room offered it at no cost and 800 people registered. The next online class they offered also drew 800 people. This time, they offered a live component, meeting twice a week on Zoom for spiritual practice together, and 150 people registered for the live component, this time being asked for a donation. A perennial issue with online courses anywhere is attrition. The Upper Room is no exception.

Eight hundred people showed up the first week; then the numbers gradually fell off to about half halfway through and to a quarter three-quarters of the way through. They discovered that they experienced the usual attrition for the group of 800 but the 150 people who showed up for the live practice never fell off. The live practice was what captured them and kept bringing them back. They learned that people are yearning for spiritual community, and they continue to experiment with different ways to create that and different price points for their courses. They offered a Blue Christmas course and Blue Christmas service that built on a book published in 2018, both online, for those who had lost loved ones in the past year, or were struggling with loneliness, and received a huge response.

As they continue to discern what is theirs to do, Oliver and her colleagues continue to ask, "If our mission is to create daily life with God, then how can we daily be with them if they can't gather with their churches and prayer groups?"

Julie Pennington-Russell, First Baptist Church of Washington, DC

Julie Pennington-Russell discovered a number of opportunities in the crises of the pandemic and racial reckoning. Both awakened the church and helped it move forward. First Baptist Church, founded in 1802, had more than two centuries of traditions and accretions when COVID-19 hit. As Pennington-Russell frames it:

> With any institution, once you've been around that long, you fall into patterns and there's all this history and then layers and layers and layers of expectation and identity that get cemented and embedded. It almost takes a detonation of sorts to break through the concrete. . . . I really think that the pandemic has functioned in that way.

The first place this became apparent was in the building. Housed in a large, old, stone complex of buildings in downtown Washington, DC, First Baptist had experienced institutional creep. The buildings had grown larger and more complicated over the years. At the same time that the buildings grew more complex, they also experienced neglect. Bursting pipes, an antiquated heating system that left people wondering whether they'd walk into a ninety-degree sanctuary or a thirty-degree sanctuary on Sunday morning, and a building largely inaccessible to its congregation's elders, represented just the tip of the iceberg. By early 2016, the trustees had assessed that the buildings needed seven million dollars of repairs to address the deferred maintenance. The leaders of the congregation were pouring a massive amount of their time and energy into attending to the building.

In mid-March 2020, when the congregation could no longer worship in the building, the focus on the building shifted to a focus on how the church could be the church apart from the building. With Sunday morning worship on Zoom, and committees and other activities also meeting virtually, the building consumed much less of the leadership's time. Time and energy could be spent on reimagining worship, fellowship, spiritual growth, and the business of the church. In addition, the Facilities Improvement Team, formed three years previously, continued working tirelessly during the pandemic and was even able to speed up their work. Their plans to renovate the building for ministry, accessibility, and hospitality, with plans for a warming center and a kitchen serving meals for the neighborhood's homeless population, a ten-million-dollar project, could move ahead more quickly, starting in January 2021, unimpeded by the need to plan around the various activities occurring in the building. Instead of the building draining energy, the compelling new vision of the building energized the congregation. Pennington-Russell put it this way:

> Anticipation of what we will be able to do and express in the name of Christ has lit a spark in the congregation. While we could have withered while physically apart from one another, now we are imagining what we can do and who we can be in our community and how we can open the door to as many neighbors as possible, which we were hesitant to do in recent years because of the dreadful condition of the building.

In addition to the pandemic blasting through the layers of accretion in the church's physical structures, it also blasted through the layers of accretion in the church's organizational structures, radically simplifying committees and meetings. Over 218 years, institutional creep had affected the church's organizational life as well as the building. Structures that had served the church well in 1960 still lingered sixty years later even though membership had decreased and needs had changed dramatically.

The deacon ministry had struggled, long drifting without a purpose. Because the bylaws said there should be deacons, the congregation kept filling those roles, despite a lack of energy and focus in that group. When the pandemic hit, the deacons didn't meet for several months. The hiatus provided an opportunity to reassess and ask, "If we can't have traditional deacons doing the things we did when we were in the building, what might God want to do instead?" More than half of the deacons, given the opportunity to discern whether they were called to stay on now that the situation had changed drastically, decided to conclude their term of service. Some others stayed beyond the end of their term, in order to live with that question, letting it simmer. The deacons did not meet, but listened for what God might be inviting them into next. And the church accepted this reality, allowing for spacious time to pray and reassess.

This same thing occurred at a variety of levels in the church. Committees and teams, now meeting on Zoom, gathered less often, with briefer meetings. People showed less tolerance for meeting for meeting's sake. With this radical simplification of committees and meetings, along with the shift of focus away from the building, time and energy was released. That release of time and energy, coupled with newfound ways to connect with one another virtually, led to the third breakthrough: new opportunities for spiritual growth. Limited by geographical constraints before the pandemic (some people drove as far as forty miles to church), the church had found that holding committee meetings, educational series, and Bible studies on Sunday before or after worship worked best for the congregation. With DC traffic and busy schedules, few people wanted to return to the church on a weeknight for a committee meeting, Bible study, or prayer meeting. Once they found themselves unable to meet in person on Sundays, congregants missed one another and sought other ways to connect. Meeting on Zoom opened up opportunities to meet at different times of the week. Bible studies, prayer groups, a midweek contemplative prayer time on Facebook Live, and book groups sprang up. With the opportunity to meet in small groups, relationships in the congregation have deepened. People who hadn't known one another now know one another in meaningful ways, sharing deeply about their lives and praying for one another.

Pennington-Russell notes, "Old institutions rarely get the opportunity to hit the pause button and re-evaluate. What a gift it is to be able to look up and say, 'God, hello! There you are.' And then to welcome God in new and surprising ways. I believe First Baptist Church will talk about this season for generations to come as a formative time, a time of renewal."

The crisis of racial reckoning in the United States also provided an opportunity for First Baptist, a predominantly White church. Two years prior to the murder of George Floyd, the church began addressing its racially fraught history in partnership with its sister church, the predominantly African American Nineteenth Street Baptist Church. The killings of George Floyd, Breonna Taylor, Ahmaud Arbery, and then others, and the resulting protests and heightened national awareness of racism, led First Baptist to step up its engagement. Pennington-Russell viewed these events as an opportunity "for our church to truly reckon with our history." According to substantial documentation, during much of the time that Obadiah Brown was the founding pastor of First Baptist Church, he also was a slaveholder. He and Mrs. Brown owned a large home in the District which they turned into a boarding house. Government workers and even some members of Congress lodged there. The boarding house was maintained by the Browns' household slaves. Pennington-Russell recounts a story:

> In the spring of 1848, two years before Pastor Brown retired from our church at the age of sixty-eight, a young enslaved

man in his household named John Calvert attempted to escape, along with seventy-six other men, women, and children, on the sailing ship *Pearl*. The Pearl was overtaken by a steamship and all seventy-seven escapees were returned to Washington where the majority (including children) were sold by their masters to slave traders connected to the cotton and sugar plantations in the deep South. Obadiah Brown sold John Calvert to the slave trader William H. Williams who operated a slave market near the Smithsonian Castle on the National Mall and who then took Calvert and others down to New Orleans to be sold to a cotton plantation.

The church has begun to reckon with this, as well as other deeply disturbing racist parts of its past.

First Baptist Church began as an integrated church in 1802. By 1819, twenty-nine percent of its members were African-American; in 1822, it was forty percent. In 1833 the church divided into two congregations, one predominantly White and one predominantly Black. The White church moved to a new location and planned to transfer ownership of the original building to the Black church. This took much longer than expected. The White church maintained ownership and control for another thirty years when, in the 1870s, First Baptist finally deeded Nineteenth Street Baptist with the ownership of their building. The history had left many scars that the two churches began to explore, starting down a path of First Baptist moving toward repentance and the first steps of healing.

In the fall of 2020, First Baptist began offering a race and social justice reading group (first reading: *Chocolate City*, about race and racism in DC), with the intention of moving to an action that feels God-led. Pennington-Russell prays that it will lead the church to a public declaration of repentance and then to other actions that

God would have them take. Having the national protests play out on the church's back doorstep in downtown DC had a profound effect, leading the church to arrive at a realization that it's really time to grapple with racial injustice and their complicity in it.

Alongside the race and social justice reading group, the staff participated in a twenty-two-week lecture series from Yale University on America's history of racism. They viewed the lectures on their own and then met weekly to discuss that week's lecture before staff meeting. They knew that the first step of becoming an anti-racist church was to educate themselves and make changes within. "The Holy Work of Anti-Racism," Pennington-Russell's video on the church's website, called church members to do this work. While they have inklings of what they might be called to do, Pennington-Russell senses, "Our place is in the orchestra, not waving the baton. I believe that, after a long history of being in charge, of calling the shots, we are now called to a supporting role, to be allies in the struggle." Thus, the crisis of racial reckoning has provided First Baptist with the impetus to speed up the work they had known they needed to do. And, for the first time in their history, they are open to taking a humble role of learning and serving rather than being in charge.

First Baptist Church has certainly not wasted a good crisis, both in terms of the COVID-19 shake-up and in terms of the country's time of racial reckoning. Both crises have propelled the church forward in important work it needed to do.

Stuart Higginbotham, Rector, Grace Episcopal Church, Gainesville, Georgia

Stuart Higginbotham also discovered a number of opportunities in the crisis of the COVID-19 pandemic. The crisis helped Grace

Episcopal Church move into fresh vision and vitality, with a deeper contemplative grounding and richer community.

Before the pandemic, much of Higginbotham's ministry focused on prescribed services. For at least half of the parish, the only encounter with one another occurred on Sunday morning. When COVID-19 hit, leadership's initial reaction focused on recreating that Sunday morning experience, and when it proved impossible, some sank into grief and froze. In response, Higginbotham challenged the church to complement their grief with imagination. He invited them into a thought experiment, imagining that they had been in a plane crash and ended up on a desert island, with no church building, no organ, no vestments, no communion bread and wine. Would they have to give up encountering God in community? Or might they realize that the Spirit was inviting them to use their imaginations and co-create something new for these new circumstances? He reminded them, "All is not lost; it's just that that is lost. And just for now."

Some rose to the challenge and began to imagine possibilities with him. Through this process, Higginbotham's whole image of what being a priest is expanded enormously. While he had always thought of priest as intermediary rather than liturgical functionary, he was reminded that his concept of priest as intermediary meant much more than what he did on Sunday morning. He served as intermediary between God and people, between people and himself, even between different parts of himself:

> Different parts of me were coming forward at this time: the anxious me, the hopeful me . . . I asked myself, "How does the true me stand in the middle of those and navigate that?" There is enormous grief, but on the whole it's been in a larger context of "This is for the time being. God's not causing this

but God is present in it and there are lessons we can learn out of it." How can I take advantage of that and how can I invite my people into that, asking them, "How are you growing?"

When the bishop announced that all the parishes in the diocese would close and that priests could make one visit to their church buildings to get what they needed, Higginbotham reflected: "I packed up the wrong things: candles and chocolate and a meditation shawl and no stole or no vestments." But in retrospect he mused, "They turned out to be the exact right things." They were exactly the right things because they fit the creative imagination mode that the parish had entered. Had he brought home stoles and vestments and communion vessels, he might have been tempted to try to do the same old thing, only on video. Instead, he experimented. He asked, "How has our sense of communion changed from a liturgy within a building to our homes? How are we tasting and seeing in different ways? We can't have bread and wine, so can we not have anything?" He experimented with the candles, finding more intimate ways to bring light to prayer while at home. The chocolates helped him challenge people to taste the sacramentality of all tastes, when they couldn't have bread and wine. The meditation shawl reminded him to wrap himself in the prayers of the congregation and invite others to do the same.

To be sure, even with the reimagination of worship, the grief work still needed to be done. Higginbotham continued to raise up the losses and continued holding the space and being present to the parish as they grieved. At the same time, his non-anxious presence served as a container for people to imagine the new, for new gifts and visions to emerge. His biggest learning was that what his people needed most from him was his presence, and that that was different from being preoccupied with a certain set of services.

As they imagined the new together, what emerged for Grace Episcopal Church? They discovered that they could be the church together on a desert island. They learned what it was to be the body of Christ in the midst of a pandemic. What did that body of Christ look like?

First, the pandemic had a leveling effect. In the past, certain members had been unable to come to worship because they were homebound or ill. On Zoom, everyone had a two-by-three-inch box. They could come to church. Introverts were empowered; extraverts were contained. Boxes were assigned randomly; no one had a special pew. When people accustomed to complaining said, "I'm not getting what I want," Higginbotham responded, "Well, none of us are. Welcome to the club!"

Second, worship changed as the services had to go online, and as a consequence, the place of worship in the life of the parish changed. As parishioners were shaken out of their comfort zones, they became more aware. Ritual was put in proper perspective, within the context of the overarching question, "What is the body and what is my place in it?" Ritual became the anchor point in each one's week, a week that contained a number of connections with the body of Christ. Weekly liturgy became more reflective, more than just going through the motions. When Higginbotham was asked, "When will we be able to go back?" he responded, "We won't go back; we'll go better." When it's possible to return to the building and gather in person, he will continue to nurture this new awareness.

In addition to this new awareness of the place of worship in the body of believers, Grace expanded its technology to enhance worship. The church invested funds in a new audio-visual system with multiple cameras, which opened new possibilities for broadcasting worship services. This new technology also made possible new ways of connecting in the future. Parishioners who are homebound, parishioners at a distance, will continue to be able to connect in ways they couldn't before. Worship has been transformed and with it, the parish's understanding of its place.

Third, community life was nurtured in new ways. Five months into the pandemic, a few people on the vestry took the initiative to divide the entire parish into thirty community groups based on where people sat in the pews, who had children, people's ages, and where they lived. As organic small groups based on natural connections that people already had with one another, their members quickly reached out to one another. Higginbotham found it beautiful to behold. The group members began to see themselves as intermediaries between God and one another. A physician on the vestry noted the deep community that was forming and said, "I want to affirm what you're doing. I spend so much time treating depression. The work you're doing, organizing people to reach out to one another, is saving lives."

This new sense of the place of worship and this new sense of community left people hungering to learn and to live into the "kin-dom" of God more fully. Sermons were recorded and sent out and became a staple of spiritual nourishment for the week. Higginbotham sought to use his sermons to build on what was already occurring in the church. Building on the new sense of community that was forming, at the end of a recent service, he challenged parishioners to call five people they hadn't been in touch with and ask them how they're doing and then listen to their responses. How does that change you, he asked, to share and to listen?

Additionally, Higginbotham produced three- to five-minute videos regularly in which he reflected on things that arose in the church and the larger community. In April of 2020 when the announcement came that schools would not reopen for in-person classes before the end of the school year, he reflected on the grief that students, especially high school seniors, were experiencing, and invited people to remember their own senior year and reach out to those students experiencing loss of graduations, proms, and so forth. The videos provided opportunities for reflection, sharing, and outreach.

Finally, the desire to grow and deepen led the church to ask, "What would it look like if we took advantage of this time and started a School of Christian Practice? If we started it, what would we design to engage the deeper level of the heart?" A study group of a dozen people formed to design the school. These questions led to rich, engaging conversations and four guidelines for it: (1) Everything would be grounded in the community's practice of prayer; (2) They would study stages of faith, understandings of spiritual growth; (3) Scriptural proficiency would be foundational; and (4) All study would cultivate a sacramental ethic, asking "How do our lives actually change through what we have learned?" The School of Christian Practice launched in late November 2020, in time for Advent.

As Higginbotham reflected on this time of crisis, he noted how the church had moved more quickly toward the vision that he and they talked about when he first interviewed for the position of rector nearly eight years prior. After he arrived at the parish, they spent six years gradually learning to trust the Spirit and to be vulnerable with one another. Then the crisis of the pandemic propelled them forward at warp speed. Higginbotham reflected, "We would have never chosen to shift things so radically on our own. We would have maintained the status quo for much longer."

Even in the midst of the pain of the pandemic, Higginbotham mused, "I feel incredibly lucky to be here. I feel very proud of this parish. We have a sense of our shared vocation. It's a gift to look at where we are and say it out loud. It really is possible to live the gospel."

Gretchen Castle, Friends World Committee for Consultation

Gretchen Castle discovered a number of ways that the crisis of the pandemic helped move her and FWCC forward. First, it shook her out of her complacency to see the big picture of what was really important. The interaction of COVID-19, racial injustice, the climate crisis, and economic inequality loomed large now in her consciousness.

Second, Friends could worship together more. With worship moved online almost everywhere, worship with Friends (Quakers) around the world was easily accessible. Castle herself worshiped with Friends on every continent where Friends are. Two of the four geographic Sections of the FWCC funded updates of technology for local meetings and yearly meetings in their areas.

Third, the pandemic allowed Friends to connect with one another at important events.

Ramón A. Gonzalez Longoria Escalona, a Cuban Friend who had served as clerk of the world governing board of FWCC, died and his family planned his memorial service for June 2020. Due to government restrictions, Cubans can't access the internet as people in most countries can. With heightened awareness about internet connectivity in these times, a young Bolivian Friend found an app that allowed him to connect Ramón's memorial service in Cuba to others from around the world as well. Over one hundred people from various parts of the world attended the service virtually, honoring Ramón well.

Fourth, the crisis of the pandemic, with everything moving online, opened up the possibility of a climate justice conference for younger Friends under thirty who met in five stages, first in each of the four FWCC Sections and then all together, and wrote a statement at each stage.

Fifth, Castle was blessed with more frequent meetings with three different groups of Quaker leaders, communicating and collaborating. The leaders of Quaker agencies, such as American Friends Service Committee, Friends Committee on National Legislation, and Quaker Council for European Affairs, met more regularly to discuss collaborative work they could do. The heads of Quaker organizations in Europe met more frequently, and the Superintendents and Secretaries of Yearly Meetings in the United States invited Castle and others to their meetings. Castle felt more support through networking with other Quaker leaders and was delighted with the increased communication and collaboration. Paradoxically, an organization whose mission is "connecting Friends around the world," which had relied on the international travel that had been curtailed during the pandemic, found itself more connected than ever during the pandemic.

Jennifer Polley, Medical Director, Northwest Pediatric Center

Dr. Jennifer Polley, medical director of Northwest Pediatric Center in Centralia, Washington, discovered a number of gifts in the crisis of the pandemic. First, the pandemic revealed the heartbeat of the practice. The leadership and staff hadn't realized the depth of one another's belief in and dedication to the mission and vision of the organization until the pandemic hit. They recognized anew their foundation in God who sustains them, and their commitment to continuing the work of God in the community by loving children and loving one another. Seeing one another's love and dedication anew helped them get through the difficult time and reignited their passion for their work.

Second, the crisis helped them discern what was essential and what could be altered or dropped. They discovered how quickly their team could pull together as they partially shut down in mid-March and re-did ninety percent of their systems, including the protocols for keeping staff and patients safe. They opened up telehealth appointments. While everything was strange and new, including ways of doing things that had been resisted before the pandemic, everyone pulled together and did what was needed. They discovered they could still offer quality health care despite having given up the kind of patient contact they had considered essential in the past.

Third, as a result of these changes, the pandemic afforded the opportunity to re-examine the organizational structures and processes. Earlier, they had introduced a new medical director role, and the process of working out that role with the established practice administrator role had been slow. The shift in the landscape helped them clarify organizationally who was doing what, and what made the most sense now. Furthermore, the integrated behavioral health program had fallen apart, causing panic at first, as the two psychologists staffing the program decided to return to private practice. But the change provided an opportunity to rethink the structure of the program and the type of person needed to lead it, and now, with a new psychologist in place, they are able to move forward in some ways that they had been stuck before. Polley realized that her blind spots had gotten in the way of making progress in the structure of the office. The pandemic offered her more time to reflect, which helped her see how to redesign the systems and thus put the organization on steadier footing.

Fourth, they forged new partnerships. The crisis of the pandemic made them realize the importance of working with schools and community organizations in order to maximize the health of the community's children. They partnered with local school superintendents and their public health department to create safety guidelines and protocols for kids' safe return to school. As a result, their county was one of the first in their state to get kids back in school. They partnered with a community organization to help staff a suicide prevention hotline, which was facing severely increased demand. They continue to explore community partnerships, having discovered more openness and imagination in themselves and their potential partners to possibilities.

All in all, the crisis of the pandemic propelled Northwest Pediatric Center forward in making necessary changes and dreaming new dreams. They are now able to serve the community's pediatric health needs better than they did pre-pandemic.

Conclusion

All of these leaders and organizations discovered multiple ways to "not waste a good crisis." In each case, the crises allowed them to live more fully into their mission, shedding old accretions that no longer serve them well, upending the status quo, and responding to fresh winds of the Spirit. The next question for these organizations was: Could the crises they faced also help with a breakthrough in their organizational structures?

Reflection Questions

1. How have you "not wasted a good crisis"?

2. What aspects of the status quo proved unnecessary when a crisis hit?

3. What new breakthroughs occurred? How did you move beyond your stuck places?

7 ▪ Transcend and Include

For years, some of us at Shalem familiar with Frederic Laloux's *Reinventing Organizations* had been asking what it might mean to become a more "teal" organization. Laloux, researching numerous successful organizations and building on Ken Wilber's work, calls next-generation, effective, thriving organizations "teal" in his color scheme. For Laloux, each level of organization, designated by a color, represents a breakthrough from what came before. And with each breakthrough, the new level of organization transcends and includes the previous one. Teal organizations, characterized by (1) self-management, (2) evolutionary purpose, and (3) wholeness, thrive because the people in them thrive and because they focus on mission.

In some ways, Shalem's organizational structure was "orange," the corporate level of Laloux's schemata. Rational and efficient, orange organizations operate like well-oiled machines. Their breakthrough from the previous level of "amber" authoritarian organizations is that they are based on open-minded scientific discovery. They welcome rational debate, throw out assumptions, and seek the truth together. Technological breakthroughs arise from an orange mindset. Innovation, accountability, and meritocracy characterize these organizations. Much of the progress and profitability of Western culture has arisen from them. Yet orange organizations can focus so much on a rational mindset that they eclipse heart and relationships. Furthermore, their focus on organizational charts and operating as well-oiled machines can further eclipse the human element and make them unwieldy and bureaucratic.

In orange organizations, workers at all levels complain of a lack of meaning and purpose. Studies show that seventy percent of employees in orange organizations are disengaged from their work.

Our financial and human resources processes sat squarely in "orange," oriented toward our annual audit that also dictated many of our other structures and processes. We filed everything in triplicate: how we handled program registrations and payments, how we handled scholarship applications and awards, the design of our database—all determined by what the auditors would examine. In addition, the time and expense of our accountant, bookkeeper, registrars, director of development, director of technology and online learning, director of operations, and executive director were inordinately consumed by perceived requirements of the audit.

In other ways, we were "green," the family/community model. Green organizations overcome the disengagement and lack of meaning and purpose prevalent in orange organizations. Green organizations' breakthroughs from the level of "orange" organizations are: empowering everyone in the organization, emphasizing culture over strategy, and balancing all stakeholders. Green organizations are heart-centered and respectful of each person's contribution. In many ways, we were green. Our board operated by discernment and consensus, our staff worked together like a family, program teams operated by discernment and consensus, and our Shalem Society leadership team and our regional conveners operated by discernment and consensus.

Moving to teal would help us get beyond the bureaucratization of our "orange" structures and processes. And it would help us move forward from the ways that our emphasis on family and community bogged us down, needing everyone to be in on everything and slowing down decision-making and movement. Teal's breakthroughs are wholeness, evolutionary purpose, and self-management. What would teal look like for us? How could we get there?

"Not wasting a good crisis" moved us off the dime organizationally. During the pandemic, our annual audit, for example, had to be done differently. Only one person could be in the office when the auditor came for his onsite visit, and the auditor and the staff person needed to be masked and socially distanced, preventing the multiple staff interactions normally associated with an audit. Also, some information was shared via Dropbox rather than all information being provided by paper copies onsite. When we saw that an audit could be done differently, a myriad of other questions arose for us.

We wondered how many of our audit practices and how many of our practices designed to prepare us for the audit were actually necessary. For example, how many, if any, of our tasks actually had to be done in the office? Did we really need to file everything in triplicate? Were paper copies of everything necessary? Our questions prodded us to begin to move beyond our orange bureaucratic way of doing things toward a teal, purpose-focused way. We went paperless with many of our bookkeeping processes. Our new director of operations, Jackson Droney, focused on creating structures and processes that would serve our mission. The board has enough trust in the staff now that, after years of positive audits, it voted to move the audit to once every three years, with a review in the intervening years. We are moving toward the audit serving the purpose of the organization rather than the organization serving the audit.

Programmatically, we began to discover what teal might look like for us when some tasks evaporated and other tasks appeared. Those who had the gifts and time for the new tasks stepped up: "I can learn Zoom," said one; "I can move the program folders from paper to Dropbox," said another; "I can reimagine how we create beauty and spaciousness in this program when we can't meet in person," said a third. We needed to act quickly. The example of the Group Spiritual Direction workshop given in chapter four, when the number of people registering surprised us, forced us to seek people with gifts and time to join the team. The example of the "Heart Longings" program did the same.

Kara Lassen Oliver, Executive Director, The Upper Room

Kara Lassen Oliver found that self-managing teams emerged when new needs arose during the pandemic. Because some parts of people's jobs evaporated and they weren't working in the office while other tasks demanded to be tackled immediately, people's work was rearranged. The questions became, "What gifts do you have? How much time do you have? Can you help?"

Their initiative to move to Facebook Live for worship meant someone had to take the lead in that effort. A young man on the marketing team had time and offered to help, so he became the team leader. He organized people above him and above them. While earlier there had been strong resistance to Facebook Live— The Upper Room had commissioned a study to see if it was possible to broadcast from the chapel, and the committee concluded it was not possible—everyone realized it was now necessary. The young team leader earned respect. He developed new skills as he learned the intricacies of broadcasting in this new way. Team members learned about how a new person can become a leader at the point of his gifts and they could become followers, even though they ranked above him in the organization. Similarly, another young man had time and said, "I can learn Zoom." He became one of the key people on the team with his Zoom expertise.

The pandemic continued to offer people the opportunity to try new things. After Kara and the publisher announced that they would be contacting all of the twenty-two thousand churches that subscribed to *The Upper Room* magazine, they realized they had incomplete contact information about many of them. Bulk orders of the magazine went to churches, not individuals, so the church address often was all they had. Someone who had time offered to look up the pastors' contact information so that they could be invited to the Sabbaths by phone or e-mail.

Then the Braille printer went out of business. The person who had set up the chapel for worship when it had been in person offered to call four hundred Braille subscribers to let them know their copies of the magazine wouldn't be arriving until a new printer could be found and that in the interim the magazine was available by calling a toll free number to hear it read. She enjoyed making personal connections with the subscribers, hearing how they were doing during the pandemic, and assuring them that The Upper Room wanted to stay in touch and would find a Braille printer as soon as possible. She became one more staff person who normally wasn't on the frontlines with customers but used the opportunity to connect, which helped her feel more connected to the work she was doing.

Stuart Higginbotham, Rector, Grace Episcopal Church, Gainesville, Georgia

Stuart Higginbotham also saw his church move toward teal. A self-managing team emerged to organize the church community in small groups, and those small groups in turn became self-managing. Higginbotham discovered a fundamental principle of leadership in teal organizations: amazing things were happening and, "If I can be a non-anxious presence and hold the space, those amazing things can take root and flourish." In addition to the organization of small groups and the creation of the School of Christian Practice, other seeds took root and began to grow. For example a book group discussing poets, mystics, theologians, and philosophers formed, which turned out to be a rich experience of reflection and engagement for participants in the midst of the pandemic.

Higginbotham noted the shift from the hierarchical model, where everything focused on the priest, to the self-managing, purpose-driven model. When people could be their whole selves and imagine together about worship and building community, energy and creativity were unleashed. Pastoral care occurred naturally. Higginbotham noted that the small groups were a much better way of engaging in pastoral care and community-building: "Curiously, the number of names on the prayer list on Sunday morning has gone down, because in the small groups, people feel more cared for and are more aware of what's going on. As cut off as we feel on one level, we feel closer on another."

Conclusion

Crises, then, have much to offer in creating the conditions for teal, purpose-centered ways of being and doing to emerge. As at Shalem, The Upper Room, and Grace Episcopal Church, hierarchical and bureaucratic structures and processes that may have once served the organizations well but are no longer proving fruitful can be re-examined and released. The crises can help move organizational structures toward new ways of better serving the organizations' mission.

Reflection Questions

1. How has crisis served as opportunity for your organization's structures to change to better serve your mission?

2. In what ways have your structures been stuck in the past? What might help them get unstuck?

3. How might you listen for an invitation for your organizational structures to evolve?

Conclusion

Every crisis presents an opportunity. If a leader can welcome a crisis, alert to the possibilities and letting go of attachments, leadership can become fresh and new again. The fresh opportunities that emerge when the crisis suspends the status quo and provides an invitation to re-examine old ways of doing things, structures, and processes that may have served the mission well at one time but no longer serve, can present a path to renewed vitality. As leaders and teams learn to live in liminality—recognizing the demise of the old, holding space to grieve it, and waiting through the gestation period for the new to be born—they can dive deep into their personal and communal spiritual practices and discern together, listening for divine guidance to emerge. When it is time, the next step becomes clear and, with a focus on mission, the leader and team surface to serve. Clarity emerges, through discernment, about how the mission is to be lived out in this particular time and place, in the midst of this particular crisis. New breakthroughs become possible as past accretions fall away. Organizational structures and processes reconfigure themselves. The leader and the organization learn to listen for what is being invited, moment by moment.

Crisis can make all things new. If a leader is open, a crisis can prove to be just the right gift to refresh leadership and organizational life, to bring the leader and the organization into new life and wholeness. Embracing the opportunities in a crisis opens the door to the next chapter in the organization's life and to new vision and vitality.

Welcome to the adventure of crisis leadership!

Acknowledgments

First and foremost, I want to thank the leaders who opened their minds, hearts, and souls to me in the midst of crisis. Their willingness to be interviewed for this book when they had so many challenges facing them showed great generosity of spirit.

I am grateful to Nancy Bryan and Milton Brasher-Cunningham at Church Publishing. Nancy conceived of this book and believed in me, convincing me that I had something useful to offer. Milton, editor extraordinaire, improved my writing substantially and kept me moving when my zeal flagged.

Jessie Smith shared contemplative writing days with me, helping me stay spiritually grounded in my writing. I am grateful for her steady, grounded presence.

Anne Grizzle provided a prayerful, spacious, welcoming place for me to write. I am deeply grateful for the beauty surrounding her hermitage and for her gracious hospitality.

A number of Shalem staff and program directors read part or all of the manuscript, making helpful comments and editing suggestions. My thanks to Winston Charles, Jackson Droney, Katy Gaughan, Michelle Geuder, Anne Grizzle, Trish Stefanik, Phillip Stephens, Liz Ward, and Nan Weir, who all took time out of their busy schedules to contribute corrections and wise counsel. Michelle Geuder also provided valuable research for the project.

Above all, I am thankful for my husband, Ken Haase, who listened to me and helped me think through places where I was stuck, who put up with my absences both physically and mentally, who supported me by cooking and cleaning when I was meeting deadlines, and who loved me through the entire process.